Note

At first glance, this seems to be simply a book of light-hearted drawings of kids and animals doing ordinary things: brushing their teeth, reading, swimming, sleeping or enjoying nature. But look more closely and you'll realize that each drawing contains several "hidden pictures" of things quite out of place, hiding in the scenery, or otherwise sneaking their way into these "ordinary" drawings. There are 48 puzzles in all, and you are free to color them in however you like, so keep a sharp eye out and enjoy!

Hidden Pictures

MIKE ARTELL

DOVER PUBLICATIONS, INC.
New York

Bibliographical Note

Hidden Pictures is a new work, first published by Dover Publications, Inc., in 1994.

International Standard Book Number: 0-486-28153-1

Manufactured in the United States of America
Dover Publications, Inc., 31 East 2nd Street, Mineola, N.Y. 11501

The following items are hidden in this picture: a coffee cup, a shovel, the letter Z, a hatchet, a star, a sheep, a fish, a crown and a hair bow.

Find the numbers 1 through 9.

An arrow, a bone, a crown, an ice cream cone, a teepee, a spoon, a kite, a fishhook, a bow tie and the number 9 are all hiding in this picture.

See if you can find two flowerpots, a hat, a kite, a tennis racquet, a Christmas tree, a hamburger, a piece of cheese, a banana and a heart.

4

Now, let's see, where are the two carrots, the hatchet,
the saw, the bird, the golf club, the canoe, the boot and
Santa Claus?

In this picture you can find a carnival mask, a sailboat, a shovel, a canoe, the number 7, a balloon, a duck, the letter B and a hair bow.

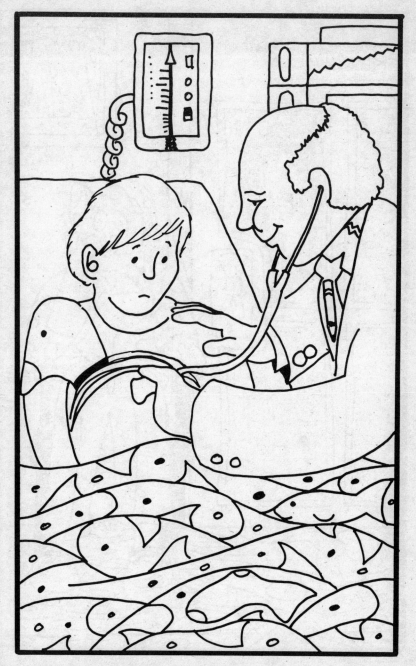

Now try to locate the numbers 6 and 8, a fish, a teepee, a duck's head, an arrow, a sock, a pencil and a saw.

The following items are hidden in this picture: a bird, a baby bottle, a hair bow, a piece of cheese, a pencil, a sock, a rocket ship, a rabbit and a carrot.

8

Now find a spoon, a crown, an artist's paintbrush, a sailboat, a golf club, a cowboy boot, a coffee cup, the number 5 and an adhesive bandage.

Can you see a butterfly, an artist's paintbrush, a bird, a rowboat, a heart, a dinosaur, a key, a party hat and the number 6?

Hidden in this picture are a crown, a saw, a piece of cake, a teepee, a golf club, a truck, a kite, an artist's paintbrush and a frying pan.

11

See if you can find the clock face, kite, six-legged bug, saw, sailboat, pizza, heart, teapot and golf club in this picture.

12

A carrot, a hatchet, a hollow log, a top hat, a bone, a baseball bat, a heart, a fly swatter and a hair bow are all hidden in this scene.

13

Now find the heart, balloon, letters C and T, canoe, bird, rabbit, adhesive bandage and bell.

14

In this picture, you are looking for a golf club, a carrot, a pencil, a rocket ship, a steamship, an ice cream cone, the number 4, a star and a butterfly.

15

If you look carefully, you will see: a rabbit, a frying pan, a banana, a sock, a guitar, a sheep, the number 3, a housepainter's paintbrush and a coffee cup.

Can you find the bell, football, pencil, carnival mask, star, artist's paintbrush, rabbit, sock and flashlight?

Somewhere in this picture are a key, a bird, a heart, a spoon, a butterfly, the number 7, a knife, a boxing glove and a hair bow.

18

Hiding in this picture are a baseball bat, a crown, a bell, a golf club, the number 7, the letter Z, a cowboy boot, a fly swatter and a sports car.

Find the following: teepee, numbers 7, 8 and 9, bird, golf club, book, garden hoe, the letter W.

See if you can locate the truck, the fishhook, the saw, the butterfly, the duck, the number 7, the ladder, the rocket ship and the letter S.

Find the canoe, carrot, balloon, fishhook, frying pan, heart, coffee cup, rabbit and hair bow.

In this one, you are looking for the number 2, a fish, an artist's paintbrush, an arrow, a sock, a key, a party hat, the letter H and a bucket.

23

Look carefully for the cowboy boot, golf club, kite, hatchet, sailboat, van, artist's paintbrush, carrot, and star.

24

Find the numbers 1 through 9.

A ruler, a snake, a crescent moon, a glove, a spoon, the word "hello," a bird, a magnifying glass, a golf club and
26   an artist's paintbrush are all hidden in this scene.

Hidden here are a balloon, two sailboats, a heart, the number 5, a hair bow, a pencil, two combs and a TV set!

Now find the funnel, hair bow, bird, bone, carnival mask, sock, arrow, pencil and canoe.

You will find a mouse's head, a spoon, a sports car, the number 2, the word "fish," a happy face, a book, a canoe and a sheep, if you look closely.

Can you find the shark, six-legged bug, duckling, numbers 2 and 4, sock, snake crawling through the grass, umbrella and star in this picture?

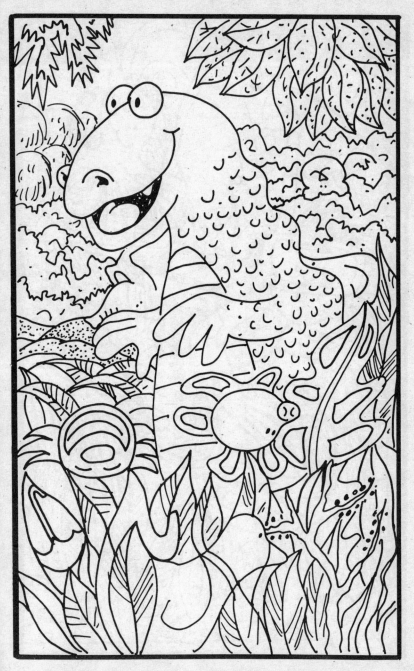

Find the heart, duck, pig's head, number 2, clown, umbrella, elephant's head, bear's head and dove.

31

Find the fishhook, scissors, flying bird, kite, rabbit's head, key, owl, skunk and heart.

Now see if you can spot the pencil, sailboat, teepee, clothes iron, van, camera, saw, hat and number 3 in this picture.

Hidden here are the letter M, an opossum, a coffee cup, a spoon, a boot, a polar bear, a pig, a pot and a balloon.

Can you see the duck, the robot, the knife, the candle, the arrow, the hatchet, the suitcase, the adhesive bandage and the hair bow?

Now you are looking for the lamp, number 8, ice cream cone, toucan, mouse, fish, elephant's head, flashlight and coffee cup.

In this picture you can find an arrow, a bird, a star, a shovel, a carnival mask, a pair of eyeglasses, a horse, a ladder and a bowling pin.

The following items are hidden in this picture: coat
hanger, trash can, housepainter's paintbrush, pencil,
numbers 7 and 8, truck, cowboy boot and baseball bat.

38

Can you find the mouse, funnel, sailboat, saw, baseball player, bone, butterfly and football?

See if you can find the padlock, letter P, piece of cheese, belt, turtle, umbrella, igloo, American flag and heart in this picture.

Hiding here are: a horn, a fish, an airplane, a mouse, a bird, a carrot, a star, a teepee and the number 3.

Where in this picture are the spoon, bone, ice cream cone, piece of cake, boat, adhesive bandage, balloon, canoe and number 7?

If you look carefully you will see a hatchet, a baby
bottle, a party hat, an arrow, a heart, a bell, an artist's
paintbrush and a butterfly.

43

You are looking for a seal balancing a ball, a pencil, a canoe, a coffee cup, a spoon, a dog's head, an ice cream cone, a sailboat and a golf club.

44

Find the hair bow, pencil, ice cream cone, carnival mask, bird, sock, teepee, baseball bat and heart.

See if you can spot the golf club, pillow, banana, fly swatter, rocket ship, steamship, top hat, ice cream cone and frying pan.

Hidden in this scene are a hatchet, an adhesive bandage, the number 7, an arrow, a fishhook, a sports car, a hair bow, a sock and a star.

Now locate the party hat, cowboy boot, knife, heart, number 8, carnival mask, bell, carrot and baseball bat.

Solutions

page 1

page 2

page 3

page 4

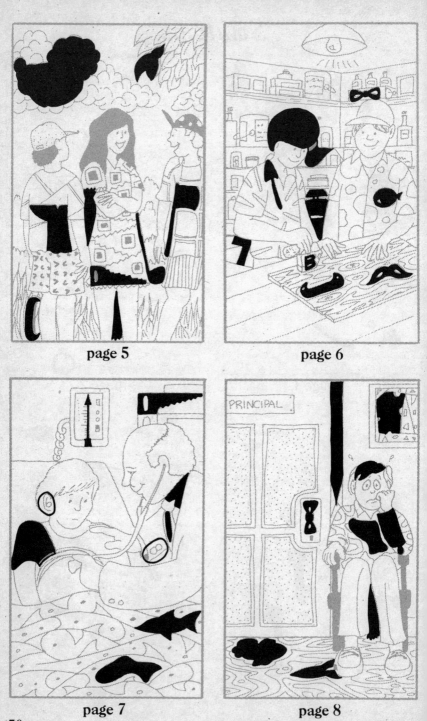

page 5

page 6

page 7

page 8

50

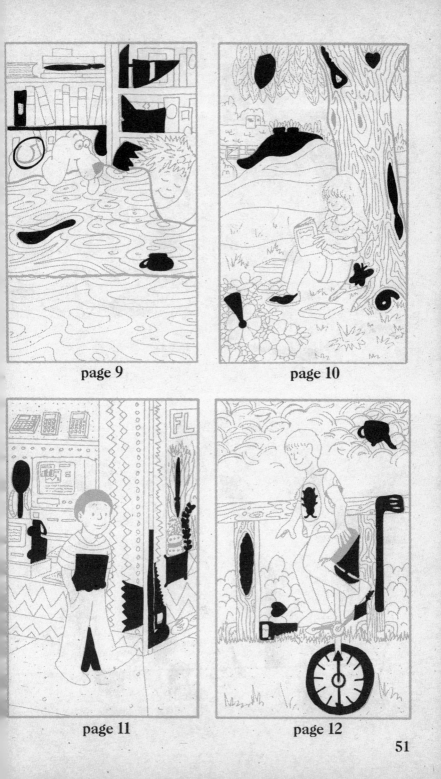

page 9

page 10

page 11

page 12

51

page 13

page 14

page 15

page 16

page 17

page 18

page 19

page 20

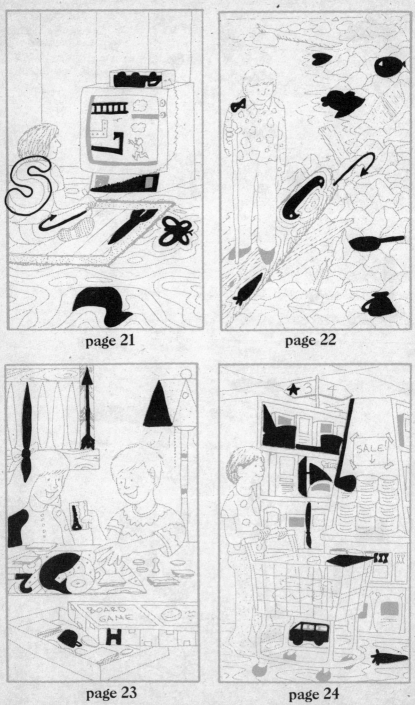

page 21

page 22

page 23

page 24

54

page 25

page 26

page 27

page 28

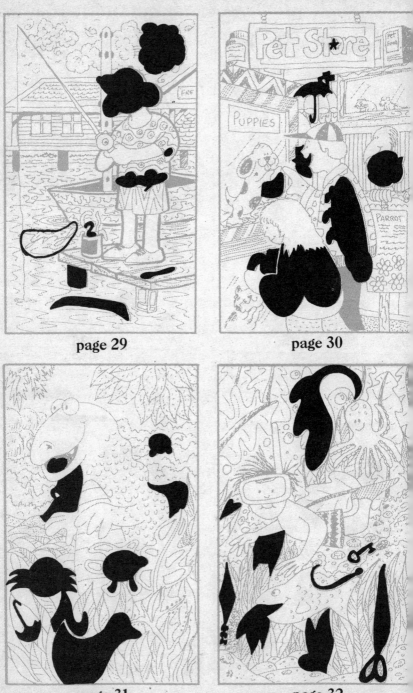

page 29

page 30

page 31

page 32

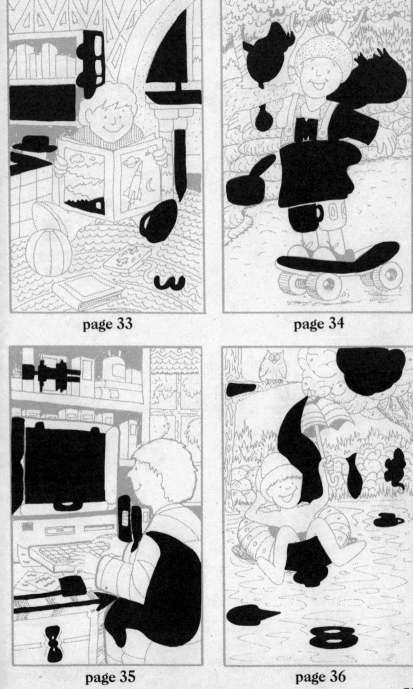

page 33

page 34

page 35

page 36

page 37

page 38

page 39

page 40

page 41

page 42

page 43

page 44

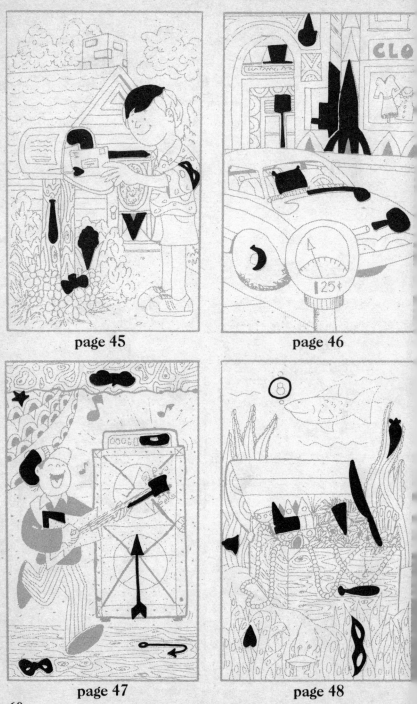

page 45

page 46

page 47

page 48